Bosley's Self-Guided Learning Books

The Language Bear's dual-language books are self-guided learning tools and are specifically designed to help young children better understand foreign words and phrases. The teaching methods used in this book allow children to learn at their own pace and enjoy the learning process. These methods include:

Simple phrases

Highlighted words

Contextual vocabulary

Labelled illustrations

Line-by-line translations

Find this book and others in a variety of translations at:
www.theLanguageBear.com

By opening a single door
we begin a journey of
infinite possibilities.

Bosley Builds a Tree House
Copyright © 2013 Tim Johnson
ISBN-13: 978-1493595112
ISBN-10: 1493595113

The Language Bear, Dual-Language Books
207-370-4298
info@theLanguageBear.com
www.theLanguageBear.com

The Adventures of Bosley Bear

Bosley Builds a Tree House

Written by: Tim Johnson
Illustrated by: Ozzy Esha
Translated by: Belén Marvizón

Las aventuras de Oso Bosley

Bosley construye una casa del árbol

Every day Bosley and his friends run through the forest climbing trees and playing games.

Todos los días, Bosley y sus amigos corretean por el bosque subiéndose a los árboles y jugando a juegos.

squirrel
la ardilla

owl
el búho

rabbit
el conejo

raccoon
el mapache

bear
el oso

fox
el zorro

One day, Bosley had an idea.

"Let's build a tree house!" he suggested.

"Good idea! Let's build a tree house!" everyone cheered.

Un día, Bosley tuvo una idea.

"¡Vamos a construir una casa en el árbol!", sugirió.

"¡Buena idea! ¡Vamos a construir una casa en el árbol!", gritaron todos entusiasmados.

Owl found a big, sturdy tree.

The animals drew pictures of what they wanted the tree house to look like.

Búho encontró un árbol fuerte y robusto.

Los animales hicieron dibujos de cómo querían que fuese la casa.

Racoon drew four walls and a roof.

Fox drew two windows and a door.

"That looks great!" said Raccoon.

Mapache dibujó cuatro paredes y un tejado.

Zorro dibujó dos ventanas y una puerta.

"¡Está genial!", dijo Mapache.

Rabbit drew a table and chairs.

Squirrel drew some cupboards for storing nuts.

"Let's start building!" exclaimed Bosley.

Conejo dibujó una mesa y algunas sillas.

Ardilla dibujó unos armarios para guardar nueces.

"¡Vamos a construir la casa!", exclamó Bosley.

hammer
martillo

rope
cuerda

toolbox
caja de herramientas

measuring tape
cinta métrica

Bosley and his friends gathered all the tools they would need.

Then they all worked together and began building.

Bosley y sus amigos reunieron todas las herramientas que iban a necesitar.

Entonces trabajaron todos juntos y empezaron a construir.

ladder
escalera

boards
tablones

bucket
cubo

First, they built a ladder.

Then they used a bucket and rope to carry up the tools and the boards.

Everyone helped each other and worked as a team.

Primero construyeron una escalera.

Después, usaron un cubo y una cuerda para subir las herramientas y los tablones.

Se ayudaron unos a otros y todos trabajaron como un equipo.

Fox pulled the rope.

Racoon carried the boards.

Zorro tiró de la cuerda.

Mapache llevó los tablones.

Bosley nailed the boards.	Bosley clavó los tablones.
Squirrel measured everything.	Ardilla midió todo.

Rabbit made sure everything was sturdy.

And owl added the final details.

Conejo se aseguró de que todo fuera robusto.

Y Buhó añadió los detalles finales.

When they were finished, they looked at the tree house.

It was beautiful.

"Thank you for all your help, everyone!" said Bosley.

"Let's play!" shouted Squirrel.

And they climbed back up the tree to play.

Cuando terminaron, observaron la casa del árbol.

Era preciosa.

"¡Gracias a todos por ayudarme!", dijo Bosley.

"¡Vamos a jugar!", exclamó Ardilla.

Y subieron de nuevo al árbol a jugar.

But Bosley forgot one thing.

Finally, he put some pillows in the bucket and brought them up to the tree house so they could take a long nap after all their hard work.

Pero Bosley olvidó una cosa.

Finalmente, puso algunas almohadas en el cubo y las subió a la casa del árbol para que todos pudieran dormir la siesta después de haber trabajado tan duro.

More dual-language adventures with Bosley Bear!

This book and others are available in a variety of translations at:

www.theLanguageBear.com

Bosley Sees the World

Join Bosley Bear on his first adventure outside the cave when he discovers how big the world is and how much there is to explore. He learns about trees, birds, rocks, mountains, rivers and so much more, teaching your child as he learns.

The Adventures of Bosley Bear
Bosley Sees the World
A Dual-Language Book in Spanish & English

Las aventuras de Oso Bosley
Bosley Vé el Mundo
Un libro bilingüe en inglés y español

Bosley Goes to the Beach

Bosley Bear gathers his toys and goes to the beach to make new friends and learn new words. Discovering that other animals at the beach have interesting capabilities like flying or swimming, Bosley realizes that he has something that makes him special in his own way.

The Adventures of Bosley Bear
Bosley Goes to the Beach
Die Abenteuer von Bosley, dem Bären
Bosley geht ans Meer
A Dual-Language Book In German and English
Ein zweisprachiges Buch in Deutsch und Englisch